FOLDER *or* CRUMPLER

WIPE AWAY YOUR MISCONCEPTIONS, UNDERSTAND YOUR STRENGTHS & GET THE MOST FROM OTHERS

ANDREW GROELINGER

Printed in the United States of America

Library of Congress Cataloging-in-Publication Data

Groelinger, Andrew.
   Folder or crumpler: wipe away your misconceptions, understand your strengths & get the most from others / Andrew Groelinger.
   p. cm.
   ISBN 978-1-7335513-0-4

First Edition

TABLE OF CONTENTS

I AM A FOLDER. 2

THE FC CONTINUUM 8

THE TRAITS 20
The Folder 20
The Crumpler 24
The Quintessential Folder 30
The Quintessential Crumpler 30

WAYS TO IDENTIFY 32

QUIZ 36

DEEPER INSIGHTS 38

HOW IT CAN GO WRONG 43

LEARNING TO EMBRACE YOUR FC PERSONA 49

EPILOGUE 56

QUIZ ANSWERS 57

AUTHOR'S NOTE 58

ABOUT THE AUTHOR 59

I AM A FOLDER.

In fact, I think I am one of the most extreme examples of the folder mentality that exists. You probably aren't sure what I mean just yet, but after I explain my theory and you enjoy laughing at me through my stories, I promise you will agree. *I am* a folder. But before I go any further, let me tell you what I am not.

I am not a psychologist. I am not a psychiatrist. I am not a profiler. I am not an astrologist. I am not accredited with any special degrees related to the fields of psychology or human behavior. However, I am a student of human observation through my background.

I have a Bachelor of Fine Arts degree in theatre. I've been through acting classes, lighting and sound design classes, creative writing courses, and stage management and production courses. The goal in theatre is to tell a compelling story that connects with the audience, whether it is a comedy, tragedy, musical or some crazy hybrid of all three. And the only way to do this successfully is to understand human nature and how to read an audience. So, that obviously makes me an expert. Self-proclaimed.

Seriously though, I have also owned and/or operated a bunch of different companies. I've run specialty construction shops that had over 500 employees of various artisans, administrative staff and installation crews. I've owned a software company with programmers, engineers, customer support and sales folks. I have owned a performance auto-motive and race shop with mechanics and racing coaches. I've been a partner in a teen advanced car control company with coaches and external sales forces. And I have also operated an 8-figure experi-ential marketing company with offices in multiple states and countries, creating experiences for Fortune 500 companies all over the globe and managing designers, programmers, engineers, support and adminis-trative staff. I own a company that provides GPS asset tracking devices to keep tabs on high-value items while they are in transit. My partner and I run a coaching and mastermind program for entrepreneurs and business owners whose businesses range from trauma therapy to running home caking businesses.

I don't mention all of this to brag, but it should give you a sense of what I believe is an extremely diverse background and the exposure I have had with all sorts of different people, in different walks of life, in different states and countries, and in completely different industries.

Which brings me back to my proclamation and my theory. And while I have no formal credentials to justify my law of human behavior, let me tell you that every single person I have ever had a conversation with explaining my theory has had the shine of enlightenment and realization in their eyes. I've had people tell me how this postulation has changed their approach with other people, both personally and professionally, to get more success. They've told me how it has also helped them accept things about themselves they fought in the past and get to a place of calm...or at least feel justified in rationalizing some of their crazy behavior.

Oh, one last thing before we dive in (I know, I said we were going to get back to my theory — just hang on). I've got a wicked sense of humor. Throughout this book I'm going to tell you some stories and correlate my theory to the 'real world', and in the process, I'm going to make fun of myself...and you. Don't fight it. Get on board. It will make this a lot more entertaining!

Many years ago, I had been at a race track with a bunch of buddies for an event we were driving in. We were hanging out in my friend Dan's RV watching *Talladega Nights — The Legend of Ricky Bobby* as had become ritual. We were drinking beer and joking around, busting each other's chops. We were making fun of Dan pretty good because Dan had a mess going on in the RV; things were everywhere and he just seemed particularly disorganized. Dan is a brilliant, successful and talented orthopedic surgeon, but in his personal life, he always had a ton of projects going on that never seemed to get to fruition. He was always jumping to the next "shiny object". His preparation was always last minute. As we kept making fun of him, he made a joke that stuck with me. He said "Boys, there are folders and crumplers in this world and I'm a crumpler!" That sentence stuck with me ever since and it got me to really think about human nature. I spent a lot of time thinking about those classifications and flushing them out (pun intended!). Here's what I developed.

Alright, now...I'm a Folder. There are two types of people in this world— Folders and Crumplers. Period. And let's get this out of the way right up front because most of you are probably wondering if what you think I am talking about is really what I am talking about. Yes. Toilet paper. How you use it. Marcal, Charmin, Scotts...whatever brand doesn't matter. The approach and theory stay the same. Some of you people out there just wad it up and have at it. Others out there take careful time to fold it and go about their 'business' as methodically as possible. That's obviously the correct approach...because I'm a Folder (in case you missed it, this is an example of my humor).

I like all the items in my refrigerator lined up with the labels facing forward. I enjoy my closet being organized by shirt type and then sub-ordered by color. I love sending my car's motor oil out for analysis so that I have actual data to track.

Let me give you a little insight into my extreme lunacy with a story.

My nephew Seth was going to come down to visit me and my wife, Apryll, in Myrtle Beach, SC. I was so excited to have that little man coming to see us. He's a great kid and I don't get to see him too often since he lives in New Jersey (where there is snow), so I am not there as much as I would like to see him.

We figured out a date with my sister so that she could send him down our way and we could have some fun together. Obviously, I wanted to make sure he had a great time and I wanted him to have input on the way we all spent our time together. There are so many different things you can do in a town like ours because it is such a vacation/tourist style town. You can live here for years and not do everything (especially if you include all of the cheesy attractions). Trust me, I know this for a fact because I have lived here almost five years and I'm confident I still haven't played at all of the miniature golf courses we've got!

I guess I started to stress a little bit about his visit as the date was getting closer. There were too many choices and only so much time.

When I start to feel a sense of overwhelm, I like to apply a process...and if there isn't one for my specific situation, I like to develop one. This of course is not a complicated scenario. I'm not prototyping a lunar landing module; I'm simply planning out a few vacation days with my nephew. But it still needed a strategic approach!

Now, Apryll tells me that most normal people would simply scribble down a list of ideas and when their visitor arrives, they would have a quick conversation, pick their favorite ideas and go have fun...doing whichever activity on whichever day they felt like doing. I think I stared at her cross-eyed. What kind of willy-nilly, crazy world did she live in? By the way...she's a Crumpler, through and through. But we'll get to all of that.

Nope, Folder Drew had a MUCH better plan. I organized a nice little survey to send my nephew Seth in advance of his trip. I even put together some simple instructions that I sent to my sister to share with him:

Hola!

Hope all is good and you are surviving the snow!

I was putting some thought into Seth's spring break down here and coming up with some ideas that I think he would enjoy. I put together some options in the attached workbook so he can check out the different things and see which things he may or may not want to do. Depending on a couple of these things, I need to make some advance reservations since season will be kicking up.

Take a look whenever you guys have time and let me know your thoughts.

Drew

The 'pick your own adventure' itinerary I prepared for my nephew's vacation.

Totally rational, right??? I mean, look at all the benefits! I gave him the website links for each attraction so he could check each idea out! I set the expectations of how long each activity might take! He can plan his wardrobe knowing what activities he will be taking part in! He'll be excited in advance because he knows what he has to look forward to — hour by hour! I mean, really, who *doesn't* send a friggin' Excel workbook to their incoming 13-year old nephew to plan their *vacation*?

Yup, I'm a Folder.

In case this part of the example didn't start to lay out my thought process, let me tell you something else that made me both chuckle and feel shame at the same time while I was going back to find this example to share.

I also sent him a PowerPoint presentation with almost twenty photos showing him all the various things he will see in the airport from the time he exits the aircraft to the exit where I would meet him.

Thoughtful? Sure. A little crazy? Probably. Folder? To the extreme.

THE FC CONTINUUM

Folders and Crumplers live at the two ends of a continuum. Between these two ends is a whole spectrum of varying degrees.

DEFINITION OF CONTINUUM

1: a coherent whole characterized as a collection, sequence, or progression of values or elements varying by minute degrees.

"'Good' and 'bad'... stand at opposite ends of a continuum instead of describing the two halves of a line."

WAYNE SHUMAKER

"Folder" and "Crumpler" live on a continuum much in the same manner (one isn't 'good' and one isn't 'bad').

This is important to understand because any of you reading this book will land somewhere on the continuum and very, very rarely will anyone be what I would consider 100% Folder or 100% Crumpler. It isn't that black and white, just like nothing in life ever is.

However, I do believe there is a 'blackout' in the exact center of the continuum. I do not believe that anyone is an exact split, even ratio of Folder to Crumpler or Crumpler to Folder. You are predominantly one or the other with a varying percentage of the opposite tendency mixed in. Even me, with all my bizarre and disturbing idiosyncrasies that I'm putting on display for all of you to chuckle at, I have some Crumpler moments and tendencies.

There are moments when I'm in a hurry; probably because my dog is rushing me out the door for his next wave of plans. I've got that one secret hiding space in my attic where I shove all of the things I can't bear to throw away but can't come up with a plan or desire to deal with. I'll hurriedly get dressed and not put everything back where it belongs. For example, maybe my deodorant gets left out on the counter. Or I have to change from what I am wearing to something more appropriate and I don't take the time to hang up the other clothes or put them in the right spot — I'll just 'live on the edge!' and toss the clothes on a shelf in the closet. This is a moment of Crumpler for me. However, my Folder nature doesn't let go of it entirely; the 'disorder' will plague me in the back of my mind until I can get back and set it right!

Before we get into how I define the traits and characteristics of Folder and Crumpler for you to self-identify and identify others, we need to debunk some associations you will undoubtedly automatically make while reading my theory.

The easiest way to approach this is to think about the TV show, *The Odd Couple*. Hopefully, most, if not all of you, are aware of this (I think they even remade it starring Matthew Perry for all you young kids out there).

Felix Unger and Oscar Madison are great caricatures of the Folder and Crumpler respectively. Please note that I say "caricature" because it is an important distinction.

DEFINITION OF CARICATURE

1: exaggeration by means of often ludicrous distortion of parts or characteristics
— Merriam Webster

Felix Unger is portrayed as neurotic, incredibly reserved, excessively neat, obsessively clean and overwhelmingly polite. He is structured, organized, punctual and respectful. Felix is a Folder.

Oscar Madison on the other hand is portrayed as boisterous and cantankerous, a man living in the moment, a gambler and sometimes a bit rude. Oscar is a Crumpler.

For the sake of comedic response, the writers intentionally exaggerated the characteristics of Felix and Oscar in order to create tension, conflict and moments of lunacy.

Initially when you read my simple synopsis of the two characters above, you might almost assume that I am intimating that Felix the Folder has more 'positive traits' than Oscar the Crumpler. You would be wrong on many levels.

First, I don't think any of the traits that define us are 'good' or 'bad', so leave that judgmental shit at the door. I believe we all exhibit traits that can be *interpreted* as either good or bad by ourselves and others, and this is the first thing we all need to overcome. We need to identify *who we are* as a person in order to embrace the traits we treasure most so that we can find the people and circumstances in our life that will compliment or challenge these traits in a way that will bring joy and fulfillment to our lives.

Second, remember I said that both characters are caricatures. They were developed in an extreme way to help accentuate differences for the comedy effect. Zoom out a little from focusing on the 'good' and 'bad' traits (your words, not mine). Felix, who is supposedly considerate, polite, clean, and organized...was thrown out of his house by his wife.

Oscar, a slob, a gambler and rude, was actually a highly successful sports writer who had the compassion to take Felix in and save him in a time of great desperation.

I want to take a quick aside here and address one other misnomer before I go on. First, I am a lot like Felix, in case you haven't already begun to draw the parallels. He and I both have extreme "isms" (that's what I like to refer to some of my extreme behavior as) that are often incorrectly associated with a Folder. For example, I am a bit of a germaphobe. As a general rule, I don't like hugging or shaking hands with people. I have higher anxiety in public spaces like airplanes, trains and hotels because, in general, I think the public is gross. I was recently at a conference in Orlando, Florida where I bumped into a woman from

Russia that I had met one time before almost two years ago in Los Angeles. She couldn't remember my name, but she said "oh yeah, you are the germ guy!" Felix exhibited a lot of these same "isms" but I don't think those kinds of things are necessarily linked to being a "Folder". What *is* linked to being a Folder is the development of processes and systems to effectively manage those "isms".

On the other end, Oscar is shown to be a crazy slob. My lifelong friend and business partner in many ventures, Jason, is a Crumpler. He is *not* a slob...although I do believe he could step up his cleaning game on occasion ☺. Jason is also not an out-of-control gambler or a heavy drinker like Oscar was. Being unhygienic or destructive does not define a Crumpler.

I think it is important to clear up some of these mindsets as we get deeper into the Folder Crumpler (FC) Continuum explanation because you need to stay open minded to what does and doesn't apply when applying these distinctions. I meant what I said earlier, there is no 'good' or 'bad', especially when specifically addressing Folder or Crumpler. It is just a state of being; of what your natural tendencies and inhibitions allow or prohibit. If you discover you are a Folder, embrace it. If you discover you are a Crumpler, celebrate it. Whichever way, you are *you* and that is beautiful. That is the whole goal of what I'm writing — to help you better find and understand *you* so you can celebrate *being* you and not make any apologies for it. And once you figure out who you are, let me know and I will celebrate with you! Just don't expect a hug ☺.

Alright, let's dig into the FC Continuum:

I was on a coaching call with one of our clients the other day. Her name is Judy and she works as the Chief Operating Officer for a very successful and sizeable small business. Judy is definitely a Folder (which, generally, suits the role of a COO pretty well).

She was venting to us on the call because she was pretty clearly at a breaking point. You could see and hear the frustration on her face and in her voice (we were on a ZOOM call, so yes, we could in fact see her!).

The source of her frustration (so she thought) was around some challenging interpersonal and professional interactions with the owner of the company, Steve — a Crumpler.

Steve is an incredible visionary. He has built an impressive business and set a high-value mission statement for himself and his company to positively change the lives of every entrepreneur they can reach, and then effectively change the world as a result. He has a global following of extremely dedicated brand evangelists that are his customer base. Everything he has accomplished is nothing short of amazing. But, just like every business, there are people involved and they need to be able to work well together for the team to thrive. At this current moment when talking with Judy, they were not acting like the well-oiled machine they could be.

Judy was explaining to us how she felt like Steve was bucking the communication paths they had in place and was compromising her ability to effectively manage the team, along with not allowing her to protect her team from course-redirections and scrutinizing feedback.

Steve's mind is always going. He's creative and innovative and his mind doesn't find down time the way a Folder's mind might. At random times of day and night, when something would hit him that he wanted to make sure got to the team, he would just send out unfiltered messages. The problem here is that it was subverting the chain of command and putting Judy in a spot where she didn't even always know about some of the communications that were happening.

She was feeling like she was just caught up in a bit of a whirlwind and playing traffic cop, trying to just keep peace and keep team harmony.

Judy continued with her venting, telling us about how the team had just completed a big launch for a new product using a new promotional method Steve had created from a brainstorming session he had held with a few people from his inner circle. Steve came out of the brainstorm energized and excited and passed the plans off to Judy to execute. Unfortunately, the devil is in the details — for a Folder, that can be bliss, but for a Crumpler that can be a source of anxiety.

On the surface, the plan sounded great, but there was still a lot to work out and as she kept asking more and more questions, Steve was getting more and more frustrated. She couldn't understand why he didn't see that she needed the answers and she also didn't understand why he seemed to be getting so frustrated with her and flippant about just getting the launch done.

We let her keep going until she was able to catch a breath. Everyone needs to just get things out of their head sometimes. Once she was done, we started to talk with her about her perspective and also trying to see things from the opposite perspective, so that the whole picture could be seen and evaluated.

Amazing things can happen when you put a Folder and a Crumpler together, but because of their different approaches, you can get a lot of friction and misunderstandings until they recognize the Folder and Crumpler in themselves and the person they are dealing with. Once you are able to identify each other, you can set up some ground rules and expectations of how to work together productively and without the stress.

First off, Judy was actually experiencing some level of frustration because she was allowing herself to act like a Crumpler (which isn't her nature) instead of forcing some of the scenario into her paradigm. The end-run communications weren't being addressed or stopped, so she was running around playing the traffic cop and doing damage control rather than adjusting the systems and getting things to conform to a sense of order that would allow her to thrive and feel more fulfilled.

She was also adding frustration because she truly wasn't understanding why Steve was getting so frustrated with her as she kept asking more questions about the new product launch. Here's the thing, Steve was probably *not* getting angry with her (directly anyway); he was likely getting angry that she was asking him questions and he wasn't sure what the actual answers should be. In the brainstorming session, he and his cohorts came up with some great ideas that on the surface couldn't fail, so they moved on to the next idea to brainstorm. Crumplers aren't often the best researchers or that focused on the minutiae; that's just not where they usually spend their mental energy. But it is a mistake to assume they don't understand the *value* of those details.

Steve completely understood why Judy was asking the questions she was asking. He was annoyed with himself that he couldn't deliver what she needed because it just hadn't been thought about. So his frustration began to build with himself and then it projected outward from there.

In this situation, the Folder needed to realize that the Crumpler might not have these details and couch the approach to get what's needed without pushing the Crumpler into a world of hurt. Judy kept coming at Steve with question after question, but she could have approached it a couple of different ways.

She could have identified the growing tension and said something like, "Hey, Steve, this idea is totally awesome and I just want to make sure that me and the team can deliver exactly what you envisioned. I realize you may not have thought about this down to the level I'm asking about, but I'd really appreciate you taking some time with me to go through these things so that the results are exactly what you wanted."

She might also have looked at the context of when and where she was asking for these details; was it in a moment where he was focusing on a different priority? When his mind was on the next creative concept? She could have then given him the option of providing him a list of things she needed to get answered so that he could percolate on it and set up a time to regroup in a structured way to get the most out of the meeting.

In either of these approaches, this would have allowed Judy to set up some ground rules (structure) that works to her nature, but also give Steve a way to handle and react to the needs in a way that is the least intimidating to his Crumpler nature.

Ideally, the Crumpler would also be aware that he is talking to a Folder. Understanding that the nature of the Folder needs the structure and detail for comfort, the Crumpler needs to accept that he needs to carve out the time and patience to work through the details, as painful as that may be, to help guarantee success.

When explaining this to Judy, she began to see my point and perspective. But she threw up a counterpoint that she thought would counter this philosophy.

Judy began to tell a story about when Steve goes on stage to present, he will obsess over which shirt he should be wearing for each segment of his presentation (Steve does a lot of multi-day private speaking events). She said, "Well, if he is so obsessed with the shirts, isn't that focusing directly on details?"

That sounds like a valid objection but let me tell you why it isn't!

Again, Steve is a Crumpler. The Crumpler's mind is ever-moving and it can easily move to focus on a 'distraction' because there isn't a simple system in place to keep their focus on more important things.

In this situation, Steve was thinking about his shirt and appearance to his audience; a potentially impactful presentation of his personal brand. He wasn't focusing on the 'details' such as who ironed the shirts, were they hanging in the right spot, how are they getting handed to him during the costume change, etc. He was focusing on what he believed to be a larger issue of appearance and perception by his constituents.

Now, in the grand scheme of a multi-day presentation where he is spending an exorbitant amount of his time presenting his ideas and coaching his audience, the shirt being worn probably *isn't* the best thing to focus on as his knowledge and overall presence are far more likely going to impact his brand perception more than the wardrobe.

The breakdown here is that there wasn't a simple system developed and put in place to eliminate this distraction. The wardrobe could have been preselected and defined, and then there would have been no reason to even give the opportunity for his mind to wander to focus on that issue. If it was already set, he could be focusing on more effective and impactful concepts. Again, this is where she wasn't working within her own nature of Folder and establishing certain processes to simplify her environment.

It is also important to note here that Crumplers don't 'hate' systems or process. They will buck systems and process (for themselves generally), but they can also find freedom and comfort when there are some systems in place that allow them to have more freedom for other things.

There is an expression that says, "The only thing more limiting than no choices is too many choices". This is particularly true in a Crumpler's mind. The establishment of a few systems to help guide them will eliminate the overwhelming feelings they will have, and essentially reduce stress.

Which brings us back to the last and most important part of Judy's frustrations and vent session. She hadn't sat with Steve and explained the perceived chaos she felt existed with the direct communications and 'any time of the day' messaging that was putting strain on the team. She needed to help him see the value of the chain of command for communication and understand the importance of some rules of engagement. She needed to explain to him that for her to be successful at doing her job, which ultimately leads to overall success for the team and then directly leads to additional freedom and success for Steve, is for the two of them to have some structured times and ways to interact. They needed to create some consistency for her to be able to feel comfortable and rely on that, thereby allowing her to get the information she needed to direct the troops.

It's incredibly important to understand the needs, motivation and nature of the people we interact with. It may be your spouse or significant other, your friend, co-worker, manager, client, vendor or whoever. If you can figure out 'who' you are talking to, you can shift your message and approach in a way that you know they will understand, which will subsequently make your interactions that much more successful. Ideally, they learn about you as well, and it becomes simple and bi-directional. Or you help educate them to get to that goal.

There is a book called *The Five Love Languages* written by Dr. Gary Chapman. Dr. Chapman defined these five 'languages' as:

> Words of Affirmation

> Acts of Service

> Receiving Gifts

> Quality Time

> Physical Touch

The principle behind Dr. Chapman's work is that each of us has different ways we value interaction. For a person whose language is in affirmation, you can give them presents all day long, but they won't be anywhere near as meaningful and impactful as simply giving them a compliment or *telling* them how important they are to you. When you try to 'speak' to them in a love language that doesn't align with who they are, your actions oftentimes will fall short of the desired effect; underappreciated or unnoticed. In fact, it can even backfire because the recipient feels like you just don't know them or understand them.

This concept holds true for the Folder and Crumpler as well. If you don't understand *who* the person is you're interacting with, and you can't grasp the concepts of the traits that are integrated within their nature, you can easily create tension, conflict and frustration (just look at the simple example of Steve and Judy). It is just as important to be able to recognize these traits in yourself and your Folder/Crumpler Persona in order to continually adjust situations to conditions that work *with* your nature and not against it.

The idea of understanding who each of us are is far from new. There have been thousands of years of psychologists, philosophers, palm readers, and anything in between studying human nature. In the corporate world, there are all sorts of 'tests' and assessments that employers give to their employees in an effort to best understand their team in order to communicate effectively as well as motivate them in ways that will resonate.

Look at Briggs–Myers and the Kolbe. Two very evolved, specialized evaluation tools that have incredible merit. We've used them in our businesses in the past and they definitely provide some great insights that are highly leverageable. In the Kolbe world, it is said that people with more than four points apart in a specific category create opportunity for conflict.

These assessments (and the numerous others) are extremely well-conceived. There is a ton of science and psychology that went into the development of these systems. I do not want to undermine or devalue them in any way, but I can certainly tell you that you can easily correlate their results to a Folder/Crumpler identity. This is important because since there is a fundamental cross between the Folder/Crumpler identity and these systems, and since I assert that the Folder/Crumpler identity can be more quickly ascertained, you can leverage this system knowing that it holds true when mapped to deeper scientific study.

Here's the thing: when you walk into a sales meeting for the first time to pitch your product, how often do you get to say, "Hi, my name is Drew. Before I tell you more about why I'm here, do you mind logging in and taking this 20-minute online exam so I can better know who I'm speaking with?" I'm gonna guess: NEVER. If you have done this, PLEASE reach out to me because I am very interested in how that story went.

It just doesn't happen that way. You have to make some guesses and assumptions of who you are talking with or you are going to be completely off the mark.

Here's an example. Let's say you are selling a piece of software and you walk into a room that is filled with high-level Crumplers to make your pitch. You start talking about every single feature within the software and you're projecting your laptop to show every screen in your software. I promise you are not closing that deal. If you walked in and had a read of the room (we'll get to this in a bit) and knew you should talk about how your software was going to help them innovate or operate at a higher level and achieve ground breaking results, you're probably going to get a bit further with the conversation.

Alternatively, let's say you walk into a room primarily loaded with Folders. You want to pitch a new idea for a campaign for them so you've gone deep — you've got a logo designed and some incredible renderings already put together for their project. I'll tell you how this one ends: you do your entire presentation and it ends with them telling you they don't like the font that you picked and you'll never get them past that issue.

Instead, knowing the room, had you come in with a pitch on *how* you will get to their vision through your unique process that allows them to participate and you give them examples of other work you did to prove your capabilities, you'll get a lot further there, too. Trust me, I am speaking from experience on this.

I've told my Folder vs. Crumpler theory to lots of people I've known through the years. I remember a financial planner that I spoke with who works with personal individuals on retirement savings and wealth development. He was blown away. I remember him calling me a few days after we had dinner where I had told him about the theory and how to identify the traits, and he said his sales conversions were crazy (in a good way). He was able to quickly gain a sense of the people he was meeting (and began to start asking smarter questions after the initial conversations knowing this theory) and was presenting his financial strategies in ways that they could relate to and understand.

His Folders wanted details. They wanted to see a strategic plan and they wanted depth to the answers. His Crumplers wanted the higher vision and case study examples. He adjusted his language and tactics to the audiences and he was closing clients faster than he ever had.

THE TRAITS

I know, I've been teasing you with this magical trait list. Before I share it, let me remind you of what I said back in the beginning of this book. There are NO good or bad traits; there are potentially certain traits you want to try and encourage or manage more so than others, but whichever traits you have, they are part of what makes "you" and that means they are all equally important. Except, well, of course, the fact that all of the Folder traits are better ☺.

THE FOLDER

Linear thinking

The Folder appreciates critical path thinking. They are very likely to be able to identify the necessary steps required to complete a task or objective. This is not to say that Folders can't multi-task. They absolutely can, but depending on the level of the Folder, multi-tasking will result in increasing stress or anxiety.

I was on a conference call a few weeks ago discussing an execution plan for a series of events we were helping provide marketing strategy with for a new facility opening. The phone call consisted of about seven stakeholders along with my partner, Jason and me. The whole purpose of the call was to review a high-level production timeline that I had prepared to make sure we had consensus across the stakeholders. Throughout the phone call, we would hit multiple derailments as sidebar conversations would arise from an item on the schedule. Some of those derailments had tangential relevance to the topic at hand, but most of them were distractions and nuisance details that were not essential to the call or necessary to absorb everyone's time who was on the call.

I could feel my frustration rising internally as well as in my tone of voice as I repeatedly guided us back on track. I was fully appreciative of the comments that were tangential but relevant, but I was definitely getting annoyed at the lack of focus. I would not say this is a result of an inability to multi-task or vary a plan, but rather a result of my deeper nature of linear thought driving toward a success point.

Detail focused

Folders have a high threshold for detail. They are strong in communication and a lot of times over-communicative with specifics.

When I say "over-communicative", you should not confuse that with chatty or loquacious (a little *Con Air* reference for you, folks). It means that the Folder will provide ample, if not excessive, amount of details to items they feel are relevant to be communicated.

For example, my partner Jason and I hired a woman, Shari, to work as a Project Manager on a few projects we had. Shari is most definitely a Folder. Shari had a few ongoing projects of her own that she would be working through while also working for us. Jason and I were talking about setting up some rules about what and when she needed to alert us to as it related to these outside things affecting her availability at certain hours or on certain days.

We agreed that if she needed multiple days for her other projects, we needed to be informed. For something that might take up an hour's time mixed in throughout the day, we agreed we didn't need to be bothered. Jason started to work up some different potential scenarios where something might take up parts of a day where did she need to be told how to address those things with us. I said that, knowing Shari, she is likely going to over-communicate with us, even to the point of letting us know about the individual short phone calls, so that there is no confusion or surprise. I thought it was even more likely that, being the Folder that Shari is, she would develop a system of sharing her calendar with ours so that we always knew what she was doing.

Folders are good note-takers and enjoy thinking "in the weeds". This can sometimes be to their detriment, because for a Folder it is easy to keep focusing heavily on a detail — that which can occasionally distract them from the actual goal.

I installed new flooring in one of my houses. I told my wife that I felt like I should be in the Flooring Hall of Fame for a few of the cuts and fits that came out so flawlessly. I was so proud of some of the intricate cuts that I took photos of the pieces before I installed them so that my wife could swoon over my masterful skills. I was even more impressed with myself that even with all of the tricky cuts around different doorways and out of square walls, that I never had to cut a piece a second time. The reason they came out so well on the first shot was because I spent so much time focusing on each and every detail of the cut and thinking it through.

For your viewing pleasure and worship ☺

Then I got to the thresholds. There were four doorways where the new flooring had to transition to either carpet or tile. The transition pieces I ordered came with its own installation hardware and recommended installation procedures. Of course, not one of the transition scenarios matched the ideal scenarios presented in the instructions. The suggested instructions and hardware were a little counterintuitive to how I had installed transition strips dozens of times before. I spent more than a week (in various spurts since I was actually working and not making a living as my own flooring guy) laying out tape lines, center marks, measuring depths of flooring, doing sketches and even doing a few AutoCAD drawings to make sure I installed the transition strips the way they were intended. When all was said and done, I should have just followed my gut initially and installed them the way I had planned. It would have been easier and far faster, but I let myself get mired by my affection for detail and for trying to match the specs.

Organized

Folders have the mentality of "a place for everything and everything in its place". We like to rely on things being where they should be; whether it is physically putting something where it belongs or an electronic file organization. To a Folder, this makes perfect sense. It creates a sense of calm, reliability and predictability. It also enables the creation of a system or documentation that won't be inaccurate because of the conformity to the standards.

My wife and I like to cook together a lot. She will be mixing something in a bowl and will place the spoon down on the counter when she is done. It makes me laugh because there will literally be a paper towel or small plate right next to where she is mixing but she will put that spoon down right on the counter. To me, I can't even imagine how that can happen. I mean, there is a paper towel *for that spoon right there!*

THE CRUMPLER

Comfort with controlled chaos

Crumplers have an appreciation for systems and order, but they don't require them in all aspects of their life. In fact, the introduction or enforcement of too many of these systems usually results in frustration and rebellion.

My wife and I have some close friends — Mark and Lori (husband and wife), and Carol. We've spent a lot of time together over the past few years, so we know each other very well. They were over for dinner at our house one night and we started talking about Folders and Crumplers. At some point in the conversation, someone brought up the spice drawer/shelf. They asked, "How do you organize your spices?"

Apryll started to laugh because a couple of years ago I decided to dedicate one of our wider drawers specifically for our spices. I had tried all sorts of ideas throughout the years prior to finding a system that worked for me inside any of our upper cabinets. I bought a bunch of those garbage "As Seen on TV" gimmick shelves, sorters, plastic risers, and any other flashy thing promising to bring me sanity. None of it worked. I reorganized the kitchen once more (a fairly regular occurrence since you can always keep optimizing!) and cleared out one of our drawers. I decided that the best approach was to come up with some sort of cradle-style system that would hold the spices in organized rows, therefore allowing me to store them alphabetically and enabling me to view all of them when I opened the drawer. Apryll joined in the fun and we made quite a fancy little sorter system by cutting the cardboard tubes of wrapping paper in half the long way of all things. (A little side note here: the reason I went with the cardboard versus using something like PVC is because not every spice is exactly the same diameter and the cardboard can flex!).

Anyway, she told that story to the gang and Lori and Carol's reactions were both, "Of course, that's pretty much how we store them too! Alphabetically!"

Mark and Apryll both had the opinion of "who gives a crap! As long as they are all together, we can just look and find which one we need".

You can guess who the Folders and the Crumplers are here! This illustrates the point in a simple scenario: the Crumplers agree that there should be *some* organization by keeping all of the spices together; however, they are happy enough to waste those precious extra seconds rummaging.

Additionally, Crumplers will be the first to circumvent a system, even if they are the architect of that system. Again, they appreciate the importance of having a system in place but will oftentimes take a short-cut approach and find a way to justify it.

Distracted easily

Crumplers have a lower threshold to resist the 'squirrel' phenomenon. I think their minds are just generally more open to inputs around them and they also share a tendency to procrastinate. The idea of *another* idea disrupting the current, mundane task at hand is extremely appealing and creates justifiable excuses for running off on a tangent.

I've sat in more than a few meetings where I was outnumbered 4:1 in Crumpler to Folder ratio. Normally, if you are in a meeting, the meeting has some sort of purpose and terminus point; a resolution or plan of attack is defined and thus bringing said meeting to a productive end.

I can tell you that in every one of the meetings I've been in with that kind of Crumpler to Folder ratio, the meeting ran away from the agenda like the Grinch who Stole Christmas. We'd be on a topic, and suddenly someone would have a 'great idea!' we should talk about right *now*. Of course, it isn't on topic, but since we are all together...it would be foolish not to take advantage of the time! The others would all likely agree, if they weren't checking their phone or taking a call in the middle of everything. I'd sit there staring at the ceiling wondering why God hated me so. I could give you a million specific examples of these circumstances, but I am confident you *know* what I am talking about from your own first-hand experiences — and you may even be the guilty party!

Big-picture focus

The above example notwithstanding, Crumplers are able to set a vision and high-level strategy that can stretch the Folder's concept of what may be possible. I think generally that Crumpler's have a grander, dream-big approach to life and business, primarily because they do not force themselves to be confined to rules and expectations in the same manner that Folders do. With that big vision, they are able to keep their minds and their motivations focused on that big picture, although they may not have the ability or desire to really figure out the actual *how* this vision might be achieved.

My partner Jason is again a great example of this.

Frustrated with the details

As we've just talked about, Crumplers are great at defining the big vision and they can see themselves in the future, achieving those goals. It is in the details of the execution strategy where this can cause frustration and friction for the Crumpler.

Look back at the example of Steve and Judy and then add in the context of the easily-distracted trait I mentioned earlier in this list. The minutiae, the intricacies of the plan force the Crumpler to stay focused longer on any one specific issue than they are generally comfortable with. The longer they are staying focused on the finer points, the less time they are spending thinking about the next idea that is likely bouncing around in their minds, dying to be hatched. Oftentimes, the Crumpler's response to these situations is to assign a team or outsource the issue and move on; otherwise they will likely be a bit grumpy to deal with.

Quicker to take action

Which leads us to this final trait—Crumplers are generally much faster to take action. Part of this can be attributed to their distaste for staying in the weeds for too long. They would rather just have the energy of moving forward, even if it ultimately creates more issues that they will have to address along the way.

Jason and I were discussing hiring virtual assistances from the Philippines to help us do research for a new product we were going to launch. The product is an online training course, and for our marketing strategy it required us to identify our target buyers in various geographies; a project perfectly suited for the virtual assistants.

We had been talking about this for a few weeks. I was telling Jason that I was a little worried about bringing them onboard in the near future because we needed to have a solid plan on how to implement them and what to use them for once the initial research was done. The next morning, I woke up to multiple Skype meeting invites to interview several candidates that he lined up through an outside partner.

I guess we are starting!

STOP. Stop what you are thinking right now. You are sitting there looking at this list and saying, "I'm organized AND I'm creative. This is all bullshit. I'm no 'Crumpler' or 'I'm no Folder!'"

Let me remind you of a few things I have already said:

1. None of these traits are necessarily good or bad—they are simply a part of your nature and you need to learn how to work with them

2. No one is 100% Folder or 100% Crumpler. There is a Folder Crumpler Continuum which means that you will have some traits of both but you ARE predominantly one or the other

3. The very fact that you ignored these previously stated rules and reacted so emotionally proved that you ARE a Crumpler ☻. OR the very fact that you took them so literally to try and find one thing that disproves your persona proves that you ARE a Folder!

It is hard to look at a list of traits and accept them for what they are, which is why I tried to give each trait some level of context and not leave it simply as a list. When I took the Kolbe and looked at the list of descriptors they use for each of their four categories (Fact Finder, Follow-thru, Quick Start and Implementor), I immediately rejected their evaluation. I flew off the handle, emailing my partner Jason telling him what a load of crap this evaluation was and how, of course, I am an Implementor and that I absolutely will quick-start certain things.

I was offended that this evaluation would reduce me to a research-based lunatic.

Here's the thing though — this was just me initially denying who I really am. I am a Folder.

I have in the past been frustrated with my own Folder nature. Sometimes I get annoyed with myself for not being able to react to certain situations more quickly; not taking more immediate action without having to research the hell out of something (just ask Jason about the process I go through to pick a laptop!). I've gotten so frustrated with my own nature in the past and had such a desire to prove that I am not "just a Folder" that I have taken some very quick, impulsive actions — some on menial issues and other much larger business-changing decisions.

Each time I have done that, I have had instant regret and discomfort. I immediately started thinking that my gut reaction couldn't be correct because how could I possibly be sure that I had all the right information to make that decision? Surely there was another article I should have read; another user review I should have considered. Each time I denied my true nature and skipped the process that makes me who I am, I became uneasy and regretful. This is what I'm trying to teach you to do — assess yourself HONESTLY and love yourself for who you are. You can (and should) take some risks and actions outside of your comfort zone — it can be exhilarating! But do it in measured moments.

This goes both ways — it doesn't always mean that Folders want to be more Crumpler and Crumplers shouldn't adopt some Folder tendencies. I'll give you a quick, simple example using my partner Jason.

Jason will put off making decisions for as long as possible with things that are not an immediate priority. But then, something will trigger him and he will decide he needs to take immediate and swift action. He had an older iPhone, and the age of the phone and the lethargy of the device was starting to wear him down. He decided to go ahead and buy the new iPhone XS when it first came out. It was a big dollar item, but he decided he was at his breaking point and was getting a new phone.

I discovered he had gotten the new phone and I asked him about no longer having the home button, and also showed him some articles about initial product issues with the device.

The first thing he said was, "I hate this stupid phone. It's annoying as all hell to not have the home button and I don't think it's any better than my other phone. I wish I kept my iPhone 7."

Like him, I was getting fed up with my phone, too, but I had been researching it for weeks and stalled my decision based on what I had discovered. He acknowledged that it wouldn't have been terrible to have known this all ahead of time, but that he wasn't going to bother doing all of that research.

His work-around these days? He mentions to me what he is thinking about, I end up researching it, and then he makes a quick and simple decision. We decided we were going to get new ultrawide monitors for our desktops (life changing, by the way — get one NOW), and he went with the one I was getting. He said, "I knew you did all the research so why should I bother?" Well played, Crumpler, well played!"

That's ultimately where I am heading with all of this — to show you how Folders and Crumplers can live in perfect harmony once they understand themselves and their counterparts.

But for that lesson to work, you have to truly acknowledge and accept who you are, and this started with you revolting against the trait lists I laid out for Folders and Crumplers. I've acknowledged that I too had the same type of reaction to trait lists myself, so I want to give you a couple more examples of Folders and Crumplers because it is in those stories that you will identify with one or the other.

A quick sidebar so you can laugh at me: while I was writing this chapter, I had to run to the bathroom. I walked past my wife's sink in the master bathroom and it was in "disarray". She had an early shift at work this morning so everything wasn't necessarily put back where it goes...and as much as I wanted to get back to writing, I couldn't help myself. I had to reorganize the cosmetics. But I decided that if I was really going to move those things around, I should remove everything, clean the counter and sink, and then reorganize it all. Yup, I'm a Folder.

THE QUINTESSENTIAL FOLDER

Haven't I told you enough stories about me? Or do you really just want to make fun of me some more?

I have a process I follow when I go to a hotel. Shocking, right?

When I first get to the hotel, I like to do a walk-through to see where all of the restaurants and concession stores are located in the lobby and make sure I know what times they open and close.

Once I get to my room, I have a regimented process of hanging up clothing and placing my other items in drawers.

I immediately move the shampoo, conditioner and body soap into the shower so that there is no chance that when I go to shower, those items aren't in place already.

I even open and then close the shampoo and conditioner bottles when I first put them in the shower to make sure I won't have to fight with the lids the first time I actually need to use them.

I open the face soap (yes, they are usually different — read the labels!) and make sure it is placed in the soap dish on the vanity.

I unfold the bath mat and get it positioned optimally outside of the shower.

I check viewing angles of the TV and select the best side of the bed. I then make sure that the alarm clock is within view, but not immediate reach, of where I will be sleeping. I make sure my power cord for my phone has a place to plug in and a way to route conveniently for easy installation and extraction.

Oh...and I like to time myself to see if I am getting faster!

THE QUINTESSENTIAL CRUMPLER

We were chatting with one of our coaching clients named Paul. Paul owns a fitness and personal training business. He's a great guy; very energetic, wants to make a difference and wants to tackle his inner demons. Paul's issue is a quintessential Crumpler issue. He might be as close to a full Crumpler as I have ever witnessed. Let me show you.

The call started with asking him a couple of wrap-up questions about a year-long program he had been participating in with us.

"How did you enjoy the program? Were there things you liked? Things you didn't? What would you like to see changed going forward?"

Paul started answering us, and literally 30 seconds into speaking he asked, "What was the second question?"

We got him back on track and got him talking about where his head was at recently. He said that he felt mentally tired all the time because he was always reacting to things instead of planning things out. He said he had decided he needed to "Learn less and implement more", which I thought was actually a pretty keen observation for himself!

Paul is great at reading books and listening to new theories. The problem is that he goes from one book and theory to the next, each one equally swaying him without leveling any conviction to a go-forward strategy. As we talked about that on the phone, he actually got himself to admit that it allowed him to have perpetual distractions to keep him from facing his fear of executing and possibly failing.

We reminded Paul that we have timeslots dedicated each month for our clients to book extra time with us. He said, "Huh, do those happen every month?" We said, "Yup, there have been 11 so far this year!" Surprised and stunned he asked, "How do I know about them?"

We said "Well, we mention it on every monthly group call...we send out emails regularly...and the time slots are posted up in our group portal."

He missed the group calls due to scheduling conflicts.

He never read any of the emails.

He totally forgot to check the portal.

He did confess that he was trying a new system to manage himself, but that he has essentially tried a new system each week for the past few weeks. This one is pretty easy to diagnose; if you don't pick a system and commit to it for any period of time, you aren't going to have success with any system. It's all just a distraction and busy work.

Crumpler in full swing.

WAYS TO IDENTIFY

I've told you earlier that the Folder/Crumpler Identity can be mapped to evaluations like the Kolbe.

Incidentally, here are some Kolbe results for interesting reference. My Kolbe results:

Fact Finder   Follow Thru   Quick Start   Implementor

Jason's Kolbe results:

Fact Finder   Follow Thru   Quick Start   Implementor

I also did a quick random test of ten people in our coaching program and assessed them from a Folder/Crumpler perspective and then compared my results to their Kolbe:

Fact Finder	Follow Thru	Quick Start	Implementor	Folder or Crumpler
8	5	7	1	F
7	4	6	4	F
6	4	*	4	C
4	4	9	3	C
7	5	6	3	F
7	7	4	2	F
8	4	3	4	F
6	6	*	2	C
7	9	3	2	F
3	2	10	3	C
3	3	9	5	C

Kolbe results from my survey of coaching program participants[1]

When you look at these results, you can see that there is a pretty clear correlation between the Folder/Crumpler Personas and the Kolbe assessment. The Kolbe certainly goes deeper through their process and helps provide better 'data' that illustrates where people may land on the FC Continuum, but I was able to make my assessment of each candidate within a few minutes without having the time or luxury of giving an assessment like the Kolbe ahead of interacting with these folks.

---

1. The Kolbe explains that when a category returns a result of *, the subject is in a state of transition

I think we can all agree that the more we understand the people we are interacting with, the better we can help them get value, and the greater success we can achieve. In marketing-speak, we say you must get to know your Avatar or Customer Persona before you can market to them. You need to know how they think, act and feel in order to help them satisfy their needs and wants. It's no different here, except that, as I've explained, you can't ask everyone you meet for the first time to fill out a survey or take an evaluation. You have to learn to read actions, body language, and intent.

Let's look at an initial business/professional interaction first. Odds are good that before you had a first in-person meeting, there were some phone calls or emails exchanged. Think about those interactions.

> How were the emails written? Did they contain quick, high-level information? Did the email get into a lot of specifics and details? Did you get multiple emails about a similar thought as though the initial thought wasn't complete before the first message or response was sent?

> Was there consistency in the communication methods? Did they text, then call, then text, then email, then text? Did the communication methods or frequency intimate a level of fragmenting? Were messages last minute or well in advance?

> Did they seem distracted during calls? Could you hear chimes from their computer, their smartphone, or their other office lines? Could you hear them typing in the background, responding to something else while speaking with you?

From the initial interactions, you can start to get a sense of where they may land on the FC Continuum. You may not have had enough preliminary interaction to be certain, but you can likely develop some educated opinions. However, you may be meeting more than the person you interacted with, so you need to keep your sleuth hat on when you get to the meeting.

> Were they on time? Did they walk in frazzled? Did they step in and out several times?

> How are they taking notes? Do they seem to be scribbling all over the place? Are they staying focused while taking down key points? Are they drawing pictures of airplanes?

> What kind of notebook/paper did they show up with? Did they just grab a few sheets of paper out of the copier to scribble on? Do they have some sort of high-tech, distraction-providing tablet? Is it a college-ruled notepad?

> What are they wearing? Are they buttoned up? Super-relaxed? Subdued colors or super lively?

> How are they sitting? Look at their posture — are they more rigid? Fidgeting? Sprawling?

FAMOUS FOLDERS AND CRUMPLERS

Test your understanding of Folder/Crumpler personas with my fun quiz on page 36

QUIZ

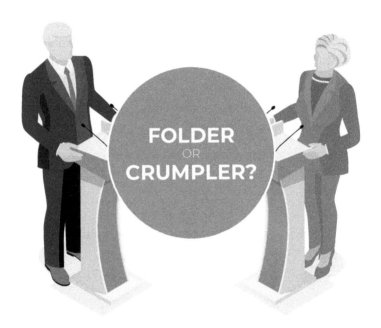

FOLDER
OR
CRUMPLER?

Here's a fun little quiz to test how well you are learning about the Folder/Crumpler Personas. The characters selected are all from pop culture so they should be fairly well known. You can find the answers to the quiz on page 57!

Presidential	Folder	Crumpler
Donald Trump		
Hillary Clinton		

The Big Bang Theory	Folder	Crumpler
Sheldon		
Leonard		
Raj		
Howard		
Penny		

Seinfeld	Folder	Crumpler
Jerry		
George		
Kramer		
Elaine		

Friends	Folder	Crumpler
Ross		
Chandler		
Joey		
Monica		
Rachel		
Phoebe		

DEEPER INSIGHTS

I attended a conference in Orlando, Florida. The conference was filled with all sorts of entrepreneurs and small business owners. A group of them were selected to present to the audience different learnings from their business along with inspirational thoughts and tactics. There were probably eighteen speakers spread out across three days of conference.

It was interesting to witness the presentations. I hadn't previously met any of these presenters, but my partner Jason knew each of the speakers really well as he has known most of them for several years. Each time a new speaker got up on stage, I would instantly assess their Folder/Crumpler persona. Some of them were pretty easy; one of them put up a photo of their home office environment where he had plastered seemingly hundreds of "to do" post-it notes all over his walls, desk, computer and even his monitor screen. This is clearly the actions of a Crumpler!

There were a few others that were just as easy. One presenter spent approximately an hour sharing extremely in-depth split-test data for his website, product launches and other aspects of his business. I thought the data was really impressive and insightful...I think many of the other audience members would have appreciated it too had their eyes not glazed over. Folders unite!

I was really taken in by a lot of the presentations. Some of the speakers were incredibly animated, inspiring and simply entertaining. Others had valuable insights, tactical methodologies and awesome, actionable suggestions.

At the end of each of the days, I would regroup with Jason and chat about the presentations we had seen. My first question was always confirming if my assessment of each speaker's Folder/Crumpler persona was accurate (it never hurts to keep testing my own perceptions!). I've talked with Jason about the Folder/Crumpler philosophy for years so he is pretty in touch with the thought process. Thankfully, I was batting 1000. What I found really interesting was that every Crumpler's presentation was more enjoyable than every Folder's. EVERY one of them. Now, this is incredibly subjective of course. There's no official metric for "enjoyable" with objective criteria that I know of, but I'm not just speaking about it being "enjoyable" to me.

Remember, I've got a theatre degree. I spent lots of time touring theatres all over the country and watching audience reactions from demographic regions that were completely juxtaposed to one another.

When I say the Crumplers' presentations were more 'enjoyable', I mean based on my read of the audience as a whole. It was very easy to see the audience's level of engagement and interest with each speaker. You can see their eyes staying alert and intently focusing on the speaker. You can see them smile and laugh at the right times and get excited or volunteer responses at the right prompts. You can also see (and feel) when the audience energy level dips because they don't feel connected and engaged. It's obvious when a speaker prompts the audience for a response and is met with silence. These are all fairly tangible and reliable ways to measure the audience's enjoyment of a speaker, a film, a play, a concert, whatever.

I didn't finalize my conclusion based only on these pretty blatant facts alone (remember, I am a Folder so there's always another step!). I chatted with individuals from the audience each night to see whom they enjoyed the most. The audience members who I spoke with represented both Folders and Crumplers so I could make sure I was getting an even perspective.

Interestingly, they were all aligned in saying that the presentations they most enjoyed matched up with the speakers who were Crumplers. Now, another interesting data point is that many of these people (again, both Folders and Crumplers) were quick to make sure I knew that they heard a lot of valuable information from the Folder presenters, but they remembered the Crumpler presentations more clearly and with a more positive opinion of enjoyment.

I was telling Jason about this little science experiment I was conducting and he said, "Of course the Crumpler presentations were better — they'll kick the Folder's asses every time!" Spoken like a true, proud Crumpler.

I've thought a lot about this ever since. I think about all of the times I have done presentations. I've done a ton of them. Employee meetings, company and board meetings, sales pitches, sponsorship presentations...you name it. I began to realize that my most successful presentations were often when I was co-presenting. I'm not saying my solo ones were flops (let a guy have some hope!), but they were not received with the same resounding energy as when I had a co-presenter.

Now, I'm a bit theatrical and I understand how to play on stage; again, I've got that theatre background. But there is a reason my degree was in *technical* theatre. I'm strong backstage, figuring out how everything gets built, produced, shuffled on and off stage, etc. I'm the same way in business; strong with the back of house operations, operating procedures, efficiencies and running my teams. However, even with my 'edge' of theatrical knowledge and the acting classes I've taken, my improvisational skills are only so strong. Because I'm a Folder.

I spend my time thinking through every action and its possible reaction and then trying to develop a plan for each of those possible reactions. I invest my time developing data points and building my case to satisfy even the strongest doubters that the facts substantiate the theory. That approach can work well in a courtroom, but even there you can see how the lack of dynamism can fail to sway the jury. If you don't believe me, just watch some Court TV for a few hours. Those attorneys are never quite as impassioned or eloquent as the folks on say, *Law and Order*.

As I reflected on my presentations and beat up my ego, I realized that my co-presenter in my most successful presentations was always a Crumpler. I played well off the Crumpler being present and could add to the energy, but it was because I had a good understanding of the Crumpler who I was presenting with so I had my plans and back-up plans for how to react to seemingly random situations because I had the comfort of my chemistry with that Crumpler. The Crumpler was able to bring up the energy level and keep the presentation from getting stuck in the weeds, and then I was able to help bring us down from that 10,000-foot view whenever the moments were right.

Jason's a Crumpler. I'm pretty sure I've said that already but just in case you missed it (because you are a Crumpler too ☺). He and I love to make fun of each other for our varying approaches. One of our favorite topics is how we store files electronically in our shared workspace environment.

I'm a Folder (as we've seen) and I *enjoy* using folders. Jason always pokes fun of me because of the depth of my directory folder structure. In my mind, it makes a lot of sense and things are easy to locate. In his approach, he usually likes to dump everything into one directory and use the Windows Explorer search function every time. I'm laughing as I'm writing this because just a day or so ago he sent me a Slack messaging asking for where the most recent file regarding a microsite we are responsible for developing might be. I told him it was likely in the "Microsite" directory. I didn't hear back so I'm assuming he found it.

A few months ago, he got a notice of renewal for his LogMeIn account. It was an outrageous amount of money (we were both in agreement on that one). Part of the reason for the insanely high fee is because he needed a license that allows him to remotely connect to something like seven or eight computers. Here's the interesting thing — these are all computers that were at different times his primary workstations — and they are scattered between his office and home office. Some of those machines haven't been fully retired because there is a key piece of software on them that seems insurmountable to transfer licensing to a new machine; but he needs the ongoing access because there are files stored in tons of different local directories, desktops, etc., and he never knows when he might need access to those files. Why isn't it stored in Dropbox and perpetually accessible? One word: Crumpler.

Interestingly, we both use Dropbox incessantly, so it's well-integrated into our workflow. Which brings up another funny Folder vs. Crumpler conflict. Jason likes to have directories that he is working with toward the top of the directory list. He has this approach of putting a "0" in the beginning of the directory name so that it prioritizes it. Of course, when there is more than one folder, the "0" folders just all fall in line. So then there needs to be a "oo" to move one above the other. Somehow now there are "++" in front of some folders to get them to the top.

For me, I know the name of the folder I am looking for and the alphabet seems to be a pretty good, well-tested system. But we share the Dropbox folders so that we can collaborate, so I am perpetually reminded of this bizarre (to me) nomenclature approach every time I open my Dropbox folder. And, just to tweak my Folder persona further, because the folders he has created have the "o" or "+" or whatever other hieroglyph, the Dropbox always feels messy to me because things are actually out of alphabetical order!

Ah, the joys of Folders and Crumplers working together.

HOW IT CAN GO WRONG

Back when I was around twenty-five years old, I was living with my then-wife in our house in Sherman Oaks, CA. It was a great little bunga-low-style house with a nice little rockwork pool and hot tub in the back yard. Living in the City of Angels, we would get our fair share of visitors who wanted to come and enjoy the sun and "stars".

I've always been a little uncomfortable when people come visit and stay in my house. For a few different reasons really...there's usually a feeling of always having to entertain and make sure they have plans, there's the worry that maybe something(s) in the house make *them* uncomfortable and they won't want to say something which makes it get even more uncomfortable, and sometimes people have different hygiene habits that are best not witnessed! I can become a bit of an over-thinker.

Anyway, I had a few visitors lined up to come to the house over the upcoming weeks. Some were family, some friends, and one was my life-long friend and business partner, Jason.

I started to get myself a little stressed out about all of the upcoming visits. I love seeing these people, but I usually love seeing people some-where else rather than at my house. See, beyond the reasons mentioned above, I have routines that I enjoy in my day. You should know by now that I am a creature of habit and my routines and structure are part of what brings me comfort. The consistency and reliability puts me at ease. When external factors invade my private space, it induces a level of stress for me.

Can I start the dishwasher? Is the noise going to bother my guest?

Can I vacuum? Is 5 a.m. too early for that?

Is it rude if I go into their bathroom and scrub it like I would after a chemical disaster?

You see where I'm going with this?

I decided I had to come up with a system to help me manage through these potential stressors. Again, as you should well be aware by now, systems and process are my "go to"!

I had heard Martha Stewart on one of her shows suggest an idea of putting together a little 'pamphlet' for lack of a better term that would help guests feel comfortable when visiting — how they can find certain things in the home and just some general expectations that make it easier for all involved. Well, certainly if Martha Stewart was suggesting it, this had to be my answer!

I sat down and created what I thought was the perfect way for everyone to feel 'right at home'.

My little document included a map that showed where the house was in relation to highways so they could get a frame of reference and get around (yes, yes, I am old enough that at twenty-five we didn't all have smartphones and GPS and the internet connected to everything we wear).

I listed out contact numbers for me and my wife in case our guests needed to get a hold of us at work or on our cell.

I gave them the instructions on how to arm and disarm the alarm so that they could feel comfortable coming and going on their own without worrying about setting off sirens.

I let them know where to find extra toilet paper and tissues in case they ran out and couldn't find them or didn't want to bother one of us.

I told them to make sure that if they did any laundry, they should move anything currently in the washer into the dryer and fold anything that was remaining in the dryer.

I included specific instructions on how to walk the dog...how to keep an inventory of food that was almost gone...to replace finished bottles of wine with ones from the rack...how to clean the counter tops after eating...even how to run the water while operating the garbage disposal.

With all of these "rules of engagement" clarified, who *wouldn't* enjoy their stay??

Andrew and   Groelinger

Sherman Oaks, CA 91403 Home: *Fax:*   *Pager:*

KRISTIEANNE AND I WOULD LIKE TO WELCOME YOU TO OUR HOME.
BELOW IS A LIST OF INFORMATION THAT YOU SHOULD FIND USEFUL
TO MAKE OUR HOME FEEL MORE LIKE YOURS.

GUEST ROOM:

1. TOWELS ARE LOCATED INSIDE ARMOIRE IN GUEST ROOM
2. PLEASE FEEL FREE TO USE DRAWERS IN DRESSER TO PUT ITEMS AWAY
3. THE LIGHTSWITCH ON THE WALL ACTIVATES THE LIGHT ON THE CEILING FAN. USE THE PULLCORD TO TURN ON THE FAN
4. FEEL FREE TO USE THE TELEPHONE IN THE ROOM. THE TELEPHONE IN THE ROOM IS NUMBER (818) 990-7565. IT IS **NOT** THE MAIN LINE IN THE HOUSE SO MOST PEOPLE DO NOT KNOW TO CALL IN ON IT. IT IS ALSO USED FOR INTERNET AND FAX.
5. THERE ARE PAINKILLERS AND MEDICINES IN THE MEDICINE CABINET IN THE GUEST BATH. FEEL FREE TO USE ANY OF THESE ITEMS
6. TOILET PAPER IS KEPT IN THE MASTER BEDROOM IN THE CLOTHES CLOSET NEXT TO THE BATH.
7. TISSUES ARE KEPT IN THE KITCHEN IN THE HANGING CABINET TO THE RIGHT OF THE FRIDGE

FOOD AND BEVERAGES:

1. HELP YOURSELF TO ANY ITEMS IN THE KITCHEN
2. BEER IS LOCATED IN THE FRIDGE IN THE GARAGE
3. LIQUOR IS LOCATED IN CABINET NEXT TO KITCHEN FRIDGE OR ABOVE LAUNDRY
4. IF YOU FINISH A BOTTLE OF WINE, PLEASE REPLACE WITH ANOTHER IN THE FRIDGE
5. PLEASE MAKE A NOTE OF ANY FOOD/BEVERAGES THAT ARE FINISHED OR ALMOST
6. PLEASE RINSE ALL DISHES AND PLACE IN DISHWASHER
7. PLEASE WIPE DOWN COUNTERS AFTER FOOD PREP (CLEANERS UNDER SINK)
8. PLEASE RUN WATER DURING AND SECONDS AFTER USING GARBAGE DISPOSAL

SECURITY:

1. THERE ARE TWO ALARM PANELS LOCATED IN THE HOUSE, ONE IN THE LIVING ROOM AND ONE IN THE MASTER BEDROOM
2. WHEN EXITING THE HOUSE, PLEASE CONFIRM ALL DOORS ARE LOCKED INCLUDING THE DOOR IN THE MASTER BEDROOM, THE DOOR OFF OF THE DINING ROOM, THE DOOR IN THE LAUNDRY ROOM, AND THE FRONT DOOR
3. ACTIVATE THE ALARM BY PRESSING SYSTEM ON AND THEN PRESS MOTION OFF. IF YOU DO NOT ACTIVATE MOTION OFF THE SYSTEM WILL TRIGGER DUE TO THE CAT!
4. YOU HAVE 30 SECONDS TO EXIT THE HOUSE
5. UPON REENTERING, ENTER ONLY THROUGH THE DINING ROOM ON FRONT DOOR. PRESS CODE NUMBER: _9 2 8_ . THIS WILL TURN THE ALARM OFF

6. Please make sure all lights are off. In the evenings, the front door lights should be turned on.
7. To enter/exit the gate, there is a button on the top of the post connected to the house. Simply press the button to activate
8. There is no need to lock the door to the garage. Make sure the lights are off if you have gone in there. A garage remote is located in the silverware drawer in the kitchen if necessary

Laundry:

1. Please feel free to use the laundry
2. Detergent is located in the cabinet above the washer. Bleach and fabric softener is located on the closet opposite the washer and dryer
3. If there are clothes in the washer, please advance them to the dryer
4. If there are clothes in the Dryer, please fold them when removing

Animals:

1. If you are the first one home or last one to leave, please walk the dog (Cinder) in the front yard using the leash. Then place Cinder in his crate
2. Please on occasion verify that both animals have water in their dish
3. Make sure all animals are inside the house prior to leaving
4. Please do not allow the dog in the bedrooms or on the couches

Audio/Visual:

1. Feel free to use the stereo system
2. To turn on/off Television, open cabinet and press Button 1 under system control on remote unit
3. To Turn on/off to watch Videotapes, press Button 2 under system control on remote unit
4. To Turn on/off to watch DVD's, press Button 3 under system control on remote unit
5. DVD's are located in lower right hand drawer unit. Please keep in alphabetical order

Contact Phone numbers and Addresses:

Andrew @ work:
Andrew Pager:
Andrew Cell:
Lexington:

LOCATION:

WE ARE LOCATED JUST NEAR THE INTERSECTION OF THE 101 AND THE 405. TO ACCESS EITHER DIRECTION ON THE 101, TURN LEFT OUT OF THE DRIVEWAY (HEADING EAST) AND FOLLOW ROAD TO THE LEFT. AT FIRST STOP SIGN, TURN RIGHT ONTO HUSTON STREET. FOLLOW HUSTON STREET TO VAN NUYS BOULEVARD. TURN RIGHT ONTO VAN NUYS BLVD. AND THERE WILL BE ENTRANCES TO BOTH DIRECTIONS OF THE 101.

TO ACCESS THE 405, TURN RIGHT OUT OF THE DRIVEWAY AND FOLLOW VALLEYHEART TO END. AT STOP SIGN, TURN LEFT ONTO HUSTON AND THEN ANOTHER IMMEDIATE LEFT ONTO KESTER. FOLLOW KESTER TO VENTURA BOULEVARD. TURN RIGHT ONTO VENTURA BOULEVARD AND FOLLOW SIGNS FOR NORTH OR SOUTH 405.

Well, looking at it now, probably NO ONE would enjoy their stay, but this little helper guide has become quite a legend between my friend, Jason and me (incidentally, I did evolve this into a full-color tri-fold brochure for v2 but it still wasn't well received!).

Jason's a Crumpler. He has a few folder tendencies, but he is a Crumpler for sure. He laughed his ass off at this thing. He couldn't stop comparing visiting the 'Casa de Groelinger' to a military compound. Proof that he loves this is that he has held onto the copy he got from his stay more than twenty years ago.

The lesson to learn from this is that you have to consider the audience and people you are speaking to and engaging with. It's important to understand that everyone *isn't* a Folder just because you are. Sharing your ideas and making people understand who you are so that they can help you feel comfortable is important. But imparting your approaches and ideologies on others to the extreme can and will create higher levels of tension. It can compromise your ability to reach an agreement. It can simply flat out turn them off to anything you are saying (or selling).

LEARNING TO EMBRACE YOUR FC PERSONA

I used to race cars. Like, really race them with sanctioning bodies and race licenses, not *Fast and Furious* style street racing. I raced BMW M3-based race cars with the Sports Car Club of America (SCCA), National Auto Sport Association (NASA), BMW Car Club of America (BMWCCA), and Foreign Automobile Racing Association (FARA). In fact, I didn't only race cars, I also owned a performance motorsport facility that built and modified race vehicles as well as did street performance enhancements and maintenance.

On my journey of learning how to *really* drive, I spent years getting coached through events called High Performance Driver Education (HPDE) events. These are non-competition events where, as a novice, you begin with an instructor and they help you learn the fundamentals behind the physics of driving. Understanding weight transfer under braking or under throttle, learning "the line" (the most optimal position of your vehicle on the race track at any given moment to get through each turn in the fastest, most efficient way possible), and all sorts of other driving dynamics. There is a lot more to it than that, but there are plenty of other books you can read about that stuff. The point is, that I spent a lot of time learning and practicing these skills before I made the jump to training for my race license and started actually doing wheel-to-wheel racing.

When you first start out, the differential in lap times between yourself and others within your "skill group" can be seconds...many seconds even. Once you get to the level of racing, even at the amateur level that we were driving at, only tenths (and sometimes hundredths) of a second may separate the top three to four drivers. This means you really need to hone your craft, fine-tune the vehicle, and use every available data point to your advantage.

Each racer generally installs a "data acquisition system" into their race car. This device acts as a data logging and feedback system with an LCD screen display usually in the driver's line of sight displaying key metrics while it is recording all sorts of other data for post-race evaluation. We monitor all sorts of things like engine water and oil temperatures, differential fluid temperatures, braking pressure, throttle inputs, as well as of course lap times. The lap time screen is generally what is being displayed, because of course, we are racers and we are focusing on how fast we can get around the track!

The system will also show you in real time how you are doing in comparison to your last lap (either faster or slower and by how much at that point along the track), as well as showing you your best theoretical lap time if you put all of your best efforts from all of your laps together. Mine would also show me how I was doing lap to lap at each turn, so I could literally see whether I was picking up time or losing time as I was going around the track at each corner.

For an extreme Folder like me, this can be a blessing or a curse.

I was never the fastest racer in my group. I wanted to be. I told myself I could be. I didn't see why I shouldn't be! I spent all of that time learning and training! Heck, I had a cool race car and I had the entire shop that I owned at my disposal — I should dominate! But I didn't. I had some races where I landed on the podium, usually squeaking in at third place. I raced in longer races (endurance races) where we had co-drivers and we placed further up the podium; but if I'm honest with myself, it was because of my co-driver's pace and race craft that got us there.

I couldn't figure out why I wasn't doing better. I had seen other drivers put *my* car on the podium in first place (there were times when I had rented my race cars to clients). One driver even set a lap record with one of my cars that was easily 3 seconds faster than I had ever gotten that vehicle around that same track (to be fair, he was a professional driver, but still!) What was happening? What's holding me back?

I had a buddy at the time that was a part-time pro driver that had coached me earlier in my 'career' as I transitioned from HPDE to racing. I asked him to help work with me to see how I could improve. He sat 'right-seat' with me for a few laps (on practice days we can install a passenger seat for a coach) and watched me without giving any feedback. He told me to drive like he wasn't there and just attack the track the way I would normally, and that we would discuss his thoughts when we got back to the pits. Off we went, lap after lap, until I saw him give a hand signal to head back in.

When we got back, he said, "Look, Drew...you're driving well. You've got good control of the car. But you aren't driving from the seat of your pants. I can see you being too analytical. You're focusing on every single turn and every single moment and your breaking down the natural flow. You are being so technical about the driving, you aren't *feeling* the track and pushing the car. You've got to let go a bit and just go for it or you aren't going to make the leaps you want to make."

That hurt. I took it a bit personally and felt like he was essentially saying, "Bud, you are as good as you're gonna get and it ain't good enough".

And then he went on further.

"You're holding yourself back when it comes to any aggressive passes. I can literally see you calculating your passes in your head and by the time you've made a decision, the moment is gone. The best racers in the world are able to make an assessment within their gut and they go for it. They don't run spreadsheets and algorithms to confirm it can be done — they just go for it and find out."

Ugh.

The reality was that he was right. The data my system was collecting was awesome and it is valuable for sure. But me being the extreme Folder that I am, I was purely focusing on the "process" of driving, thinking back to the theoretical best lines I learned about during my HPDE days. I was staring at the "plus" and "minus" of each fraction of a second through every corner and not letting go enough to look down the track and just *drive*.

I tried to become more impulsive. I pushed the car and myself harder and tried to ignore what I had done in the past at each corner. And you know what happened? I felt insanely uncomfortable. And I crashed — a bunch of times. I wasn't being true to who I was and I was creating havoc...and a lot of expense!

Now at the same time, my shop had two race cars. While I was trying to get better at sprint racing (the shorter races where it is just one driver per car racing), we started campaigning the cars in endurance races (the ones I mentioned earlier where we have co-drivers because the races are 4, 6, 12 or even 24 hours long).

I started really enjoying the endurance racing (we call them enduros) over the sprint races. In the enduros, it is rarely the car with the fastest lap times that wins because there is so much more preparation and strategy that plays into the win. Is the race car even prepped properly to last the full race? How quickly can you do your fuel stops? How fast can you change your drivers? Did you time your tire changes correctly? There are a million details that go into endurance racing victories and I'd argue that only half of the win comes from the drivers. Sure, you need them to be reasonably quick and not hit anything, but on a track where the lap time is under 2 minutes and only fractions of a second separate the winners, an extra 20 seconds in the pits due to an error can be insurmountable. Plus, sometimes speed isn't your friend. It burns gas, and depending on where you are in the race, you may not want to be doing your fastest laps because you'd rather lose 1 second per lap than stop for a mandatory 5-minute fueling pit stop. Who's making those decisions? Not the driver — it was the race strategist!

My shop and race team started doing more and more endurance races; partly because they were much more profitable for our shop but partly because I loved them so much more. In most of our enduros, we would put three drivers per car, so we would rent out 3 'seats' per car. I stopped driving and rented out my seat as well because I realized I was a significantly better strategist than I was a driver. I had learned that there were always going to be better drivers than me but there weren't many strategists better than me!

I developed all sorts of processes and checklists to make sure those cars were ready. My mechanics had clear deadlines and expectations. I had all of the spares ready and organized. Our rolling toolboxes looked like they were display cases for Lowes or Home Depot because they were so organized. I would sit at the control tent and communicate with the drivers in both cars on radio while I ran fuel strategy scenarios and kept an eye on the other teams to keep ahead of any strategy changes they made. And we had wins — and who doesn't like winning?

See, once I accepted who I was and came to peace with it, I really enjoyed what I was doing and how I was doing it. It took the frustrations I was having with a hobby (and lifestyle at that point) and turned them into feelings of accomplishment and satisfaction.

The same has been true through my professional career. Jason and I always joke that we are each our "longest lasting successful relationship". We've had first wives, friends and other business partners come and go, but we have known each other for nearly 40 years and we are still friends who work together.

Jason is most definitely a Crumpler like I've mentioned before, but I have found how his Crumpler ways and strengths have balanced me and enabled me to find some of the greatest successes I have had in my career(s).

I am extremely strong with tactics. I live for systems, processes, optimizations, efficiencies. I like to think I have pretty good interpersonal skills and feedback from my teams has always been that they enjoy my leadership. But I'm not strong on taking the quickest action all of the time. I can see strategic goals, but I hold myself back from daring to dream the biggest vision. When I start to paint those pictures, I begin to think about the details and what it will take and the tactics get in the way of that bigger picture.

Jason, in his Crumpler way, has great strength in being able to not worry or bother thinking about those details when they don't even matter yet. We always tell our coaching clients you need to figure out "first *why*, then *how*". You need to set your sights on whatever glorious destination you want to get to before you ever worry about how you are going to get there. I know this theory in concept and, like I said, I preach it all the time. I also know that my Folder persona gets in my own way.

That's why he and I make such a strong team. In the businesses I have owned and operated on my own, I have had some home runs but no grand slams. My businesses always had Standard Operating

Procedures, even when I was just a company of one because I knew at some point I was going to either hire people full time or use freelancers. I documented everything I did right from the get-go, even if it was just how I used Stamps.com to ship a package. I had all the forms and flow charts ready and when I brought new people in, it made defining their roles easy and training a breeze. But I never dominated my industries the way I know my companies could and should have because I couldn't step beyond my own limiting beliefs and constraints to really define and champion a Big Hairy Audacious Goal[2].

Jason sees it from the other side. His Crumpler persona allows him to dream big and advocate hard for that vision. Jason started a company in New Jersey back in 1997 as a systems integration business. The company originally focused on providing audio, lighting and low voltage system design and installation for the retail and hospitality industries. He enjoyed the work but knew that no matter how well his company performed, they would always be positioned a little too low on the totem pole and viewed more as a vendor and commodity than as a strategic partner and visionary. Jason had a goal and a vision of elevating the company to an international brand that was compensated based on value and not just a mark-up of goods and services.

I was working in Los Angeles at the time and he called and told me he wanted me to come work with him. He explained his vision and said that he not only believed it was possible, but that he *knew* it was possible, especially if I were to come on board.

When I started, we were a respectable small business with about twelve employees and revenues that had just broken through the seven-figure mark. Over the next seven years, we grew to a team of hundreds with offices across the US and overseas. We had become a premier thought leader in the Experiential Marketing space, a category that we helped create and define thanks to Jason's vision. We ultimately

---

2. *Built to Last: Successful Habits of Visionary Companies* by James Collins and Jerry Porras

successfully exited the business by selling the entity to a Private Equity group for an impressive amount.

How did it all happen? It happened by combining the power and strengths of a Crumpler and a Folder. Jason set some outrageous goals and was never willing to waver from them. He didn't worry all the time about *how* we were going to achieve it because that was on me. Knowing the vision, I was able to layout the processes, the structures, and the systems that were going to enable us to scale and succeed. We did.

EPILOGUE

Jason and I decided to help out a friend, Erik, who was trying to do a launch of an online course. Erik has a great idea but he is a Crumpler to the extreme. He could not figure out how to get his launch materials together, scheduled and executed even when he had the plans literally handed to him. This man is the KING of distraction and focus-deficit. He's always running from one meeting to the next and traveling the globe, but he never took any of the down time to *plan ahead* and come up with a strategy. He kept getting more and more depressed about how he had all of these people excited about his course but they just couldn't buy it because he hadn't finished putting the funnel and offer together.

We felt bad for him; he's a really great guy and we want to see him succeed. We decided we would help him out since a "done with you" model wasn't working well and he just needed a "done for you" approach ASAP.

As we were putting together the initial proposal of how we were going to help Erik, Jason and I were talking about how this could potentially be a product offering we provide to others if we put the right team together. There are a lot of people we know in the same boat as Erik; great ideas and product but without enough focus or ability to execute. We decided to keep that thought in the back of our mind as we helped Erik out on this project.

I was chatting with Jason the other day as he was working on a few of the behind-the-scenes things for Erik's launch. I asked him if he was screen capturing or documenting the steps he was doing in case we decided to pursue this business segment.

Crickets.

See, sometimes this Folder is as good for that Crumpler as he is for me ☺.

QUIZ ANSWERS

Presidential	Folder	Crumpler
Donald Trump		✔
Hillary Clinton	✔	

The Big Bang Theory	Folder	Crumpler
Sheldon	✔	
Leonard	✔	
Raj	✔	
Howard		✔
Penny		✔

Seinfeld	Folder	Crumpler
Jerry	✔	
George		✔
Kramer		✔
Elaine	✔	

Friends	Folder	Crumpler
Ross	✔	
Chandler	✔	
Joey		✔
Monica	✔	
Rachel		✔
Phoebe		✔

AUTHOR'S NOTE

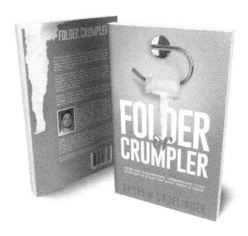

Thanks for reading! If you enjoyed this book or found it useful I'd be very grateful if you'd post a short review on Amazon. Your support really does make a difference and I read all the reviews personally so I can get your feedback and make this book even better.

Thanks again for your support!

ABOUT THE AUTHOR

Andrew is an entrepreneurial coach and business owner. He's also a creative at heart and earned his degree in theater from Carnegie Mellon University. He has working knowledge in acting theory, lighting and sound design, creative storytelling, and stage management. He finds this background incredibly useful in running a successful business and connecting with his customers.

Andrew has owned and operated several companies over the years in industries ranging from specialty construction shops to software development. Now, he runs a company that offers innovative entrepreneurial training programs to business owners. He also writes books sometimes. When he's not working or writing, Andrew likes to run marathons.

He currently resides in South Carolina with his wife, Apryll, and their giant, slobbery Neapolitan Mastiff, Dino.

> **Find out more at www.foldercrumpler.com**

CPSIA information can be obtained
at www.ICGtesting.com
Printed in the USA
FFHW010215220119
502162965-5192FF

9 781733 551304